American Criminology

A Mini Course

by

JJ Botta

American Criminology

ISBN: 978-0-359-49598-6

McGraw-Hill Open-Publishing

Acknowledgements

I wish to thank my Professors at New York Law School for helping me to appreciate criminological theories and their significance to the future of criminal justice.

Dedication

This book is dedicated to my wife, Carol, who has never failed to support me in my writing and teaching ventures.

Table of Contents

Charles Darwin

Introduction

The twenty-first century brought with it major changes in the ideological approaches to crime and crime causation. The variations in thinking in the United States regarding the reasons for criminal behavior emanate from the mythology of the American people. In the last century, the work *myth* was often interpreted to mean falsity. Traditionally, however, a myth is defined as a controlling idea or belief, whether true or false. When groups of related myths connect, a mythology results. Thus, when the mindset of a societal group is fixed upon a theory of crime causation, the theory is adopted and reflected in law, criminal procedure, and crime punishment.

Criminology is the scientific study of crime, crime causation, and criminal behavior. Despite this generally accepted definition, critics challenge the usefulness of studying crime phenomena and the accuracy of labeling the discipline a *science,* since criminology provides no definitive answers. Crime causation theories and preventive methodologies are not consistent. Criminological findings change with societal mythologies.

There is a modern trend toward assessing reasons for criminal behavior in the context of scientific thought, because collectively people in society would love to believe there is a cure for criminal behavior. For practical purposes, criminal investigation probes criminal behavior, the causes of such behavior, and societal reaction to criminal activity.

The real benefit of criminology as a discipline lies in the understanding of the theories propounded by scholars to explain crime in hopes of discovering adequate ways of dealing with the societal problem through prevention and control. Assistance to victims and treatment of offenders varies with societal attitudes. It is highly unlikely the crime problem will be solved by some scientific formula. Thus, societies must explore potential means through which people can interrelate more harmoniously and by which those who do not can be ethically treated. Studying relevant theories helps to spawn acceptable societal solutions to dealing with the problem of crime.

One of the greatest difficulties in approaching the discipline of criminology lies in the very definitions of crime and criminal behavior. From a sociological perspective, criminologists seek to discover why people act in ways harmful to societal interests. Since criminology is a social science, it concerns itself with both social and individual causes of criminal behavior. From a legal perspective, however, criminologists view crime as an act that violates some statutory scheme outlining prohibited behavior and assessing penalties for such behavior. In other words, legally there is no crime if there is no law preventing the behavior. From the societal vantage point, many people commit acts inconsistent with American mythology, but they are not considered crimes. Likewise, many people arrested for crimes have committed acts that American mythology favors. Still others commit wrongful acts and are never apprehended, thereby denying society the right to judge whether the acts were or were not criminal.

There is quite a difference between the application of a strict legal definition of crime that presupposes a conviction and a sociological study of the act in relation to societal interests. For example, suppose a young man were to buy a gun and use it to commit an armed robbery of a local establishment in his hometown. Suppose further he was acquitted at trial on a legal technicality. Has he committed a crime? Not legally. The victimized store clerk might be permanently adversely affected by the young man's behavior. Society has been harmed, yet there is no crime. Obviously from the criminal justice perspective, society must deal with the system of laws, the procedures of law enforcement, the court system, and correctional institutions. But criminologists from an academic vantage point must be more concerned with the underlying reason for the young man's behavior than the operation of the societal organizations established to deal with that behavior. By understanding the actions harmful to society, the actors who have caused the harm, and the reasons for those actions, society derives an enormous benefit from the discipline aimed at preventing such actions in the future. The definition of crime is secondary. The focus is on the behavior deemed unacceptable by society.

In American society, crime is broadly characterized into two types: *mala in se* crime and *mala prohibita* crime. Mala in se acts are considered morally wrong inn society, despite the fact that definitions of morality vary greatly. Nevertheless, crimes like robbery and rape are deemed wrong in and of themselves applying most moral standards, and thus become criminal by their nature. Mala prohibita crimes, on the other hand, are crimes because we say they are crimes. Legislative restrictions declare certain acts illegal even though they are not considered by most in society to be morally reprehensible. For example, speeding might be against the law, but the ticket is issued by legislative directive, not societal moral outrage. Obviously, the penalties for criminal behavior might have a wide range, with the greater emphasis for punishment on the mala in se types.

In the United States, there are currently two major divisions of mythological thought pertaining to American society's approach toward crime. *Under-criminalization* is the term applied to a criminal justice system whereby the criminal laws fail to adequately prohibit those actions most people generally believe to be mala in se crime. An example of under-criminalization might be a legislative failure to prohibit the dispensing of pornographic material to children. *Over-criminalization* is the term applied to a criminal justice system whereby the legislators responsible for the creation of criminal laws are believed by most to be legislating morality for the populace, with no clear victim delineated in the laws passed. An example of over-criminalization might be legislation that prohibits the personal use of marijuana.

Crime is most often associated with behavior that is deviant. By deviance, criminologists generally mean behavior that violated the cultural norms of society. It is behavior outside the range of normal societal toleration. As such, deviance covers a wide area of activity that might stretch from the extremely dangerous to the moderately annoying. Thus, most criminologists assert that some forms of crime are not deviant. What is clear, however, is that deviance is relative to time, place, and the people making such evaluations. It appears, therefore, that behavior unacceptable as deviant depends largely on cultural values and norms.

Once again, the definition is problematic because, as we have seen, some behavior most of us would consider outside societal norms has not been declared criminal by legislatures, and some behavior most of us would consider normal in society has been outlawed. Thus, to conclude all criminal behavior is deviant is a misstatement. Likewise, to conclude all deviant behavior has been outlawed is equally false. For criminologists to determine the extent of deviant behavior, they must first define societal norms. The problem is far more complex than it appears at first glance. Consider, for example, the natural act of breastfeeding. While most would be hard pressed to assert the act as abnormal, breastfeeding in public is considered criminal behavior in many states. The issue in the criminal justice arena is viewed from the perspective of the statutes passed requiring or prohibiting certain behavior. The issue from the sociological perspective deals with the act as a societal norm.

Consider further some very normal acts most of us would deem amoral, or having no particular moral consequence, such as getting dressed each morning. Nevertheless, it has become the societal norm in most countries to wear clothing in public. Therefore, legislatures have mandated the wearing of clothing in public, not because failure to do so is mala in se crime, but because it is prohibited as a violation of societal norms.

One can readily see the connection between criminology and the criminal justice system. The study of crime and crime causation necessarily impacts upon society's view of norms and abnormal behavior. In studying criminology and collecting related statistical data, experts must blend theoretical data from many disciplines to thoroughly explore common societal activities, their participants, and their causes. Psychology, sociology, biology, philosophy, penology, and even economics must be considered to gather the most accurate data applying critical thinking processes. Thus, criminologists must approach the subject matter from a theoretical position, explaining the reasons for criminal behavior, while differentiating such actions from non-criminal behavior.

In the following chapters, we will approach criminology from the sociological perspective. More precisely, we will consider the most popular theoretical applications and their greatest components. Unfortunately, theory is the best evidence the *science* of criminology can offer. This tends to be less than satisfying. Nevertheless, the study has major significance. The theoretical conclusions reached by criminologists heavily influence mythologies in societies, especially in American society, which is the focus of this mini course. For example, when criminologists conclude social policies constitute the underlying causes of certain kinds of unacceptable societal behavior, people tend to weigh those conclusions while formulating their personal opinions. Should major criminological studies conclude *guns cause crime,* the American public is likely to adopt the findings as scientific. Should the finding lead to the *people kill people* conclusion, the mythology is likely to change accordingly. It is of paramount importance, therefore, to study the most significant and influential theories promoted in order to draw from the most accurate material available in formulating opinions as to crime and deviance, or normalcy and abnormality in American society.

One significant consideration before any in-depth discussion of major criminological theories and theorists is the competition between two social and political aspects of American society: the *social problems perspective* and the *social responsibility perspective.*

Those viewing criminology from the social problems perspective assert that crime is primarily a manifestation of underlying social problems. These problems, such as poverty, racial and gender discrimination, inadequate educational systems, and the breakdown of long-standing social institutions like marriage, family, and religion, produce criminal activity. In other words, crime is tantamount to a public health concern and should be treated as such. Therefore, since crime is an outgrowth of social conditions, increased social programs and economic opportunities provide solutions to crime. Proponents of this mythology see a strong connection between crime and social problems.

As an alternative approach, proponents of the social responsibility perspective hold individual perpetrators responsible for their acts of crime. Those advancing this viewpoint believe crime is primarily committed because it is simply easier than conformity. Accordingly, social programs do little to negate the causes of crime because criminals refusing to conform, opting for the excitement of crime, will more often act irresponsibly in society. Crime, therefore, is the result of actions by those not socially responsible, necessitating the wider use of police power and the passage of tougher criminal punishments.

It is important to realize the absence of a single criminological mythology in the United States today. Our nation is philosophically divided on the purpose of criminological study, under and over-criminalization, and social problems and social responsibility perspectives toward crime. As we shall see, modern approaches toward criminological studies are moving in the direction of broader sociological cohesion.

Important Concepts to Explore

Criminology: Criminology is the scientific study of crime, crime causation, and criminal behavior.

Demonological Theory: A loosely organized system of criminological thought that gained a great deal of notoriety due in large part to religious and theological explanations for societal behavior considered deviant.

Classical Theory: With a focus on individuals, these theories suggest that since human beings are rational, crime is a matter of free will and punishments should proportionately fit the crimes.

Neoclassical Theory: With more concentration on crimes than individuals, these theories are a continuation of classical thinking, with a focus on individual rights and due process of law. They suggest individuals do not act by free will when committing crimes. Neoclassical theory admits environmental, psychological, and other mitigating or extenuating circumstances as modifying conditions to the classical theory.

Positivist Theory: These theories are the opposite of classical theories. They suggest that punishment for acts beyond the control of the actors is unethical. Proponents stressed crime prevention, rather than crime punishment.

Psychological Theory: Deviant behavior is symptomatic of deep-rooted psychological problems, which may be treated with psychotherapy.

Economic Theory: This is the belief that economic disparity is the leading factor in criminal behavior.

Ecological Theory: Ecological criminologists search for the causes of crime in the interrelationships among human beings as biological organisms and their physical environments.

Biological Theory: Modern criminologists and sociologists argue that humane governments must not punish human beings biologically incapable of acceptable social behavior.

Sociological Theories: From a sociological perspective, segments of American society view crime as a means to attain success among those economically deprived.

Anomie Theory: Theorists suggest that people deprived of legitimate opportunities to succeed in their communities turn to illegitimate opportunities provided by subcultures, which rely on deviant behavioral patterns to realize their aspirations.

Social Process Theories: These theories suggest that crime is due more to social disorganization than to abnormal individuals participating in deviant behavior.

Social Control Theories: Those subscribing to such theories assert that the methods of social control established in a civilized society determine whether people will either conform or become deviant.

Critical Theories: Unlike sociological theories, when searching for crime causation critical theories focus on society as the unit of analysis, not the individuals comprising society.

Conflict Theory: Conflict criminologists view societies as characteristic of the struggle for dominance among competing groups and institutions.

Labeling Theory: Labeling theoretical approaches to crime assume that societies designate segments of the population as deviant.

Radical Criminological Theory: Radical theorists believe individual competition for economic gain encourages crime.

Lesson 1: Early Criminological Thought

An historical treatment of criminological thought is essential to a thorough understanding of the modern theories to be covered in this mini course. While we cannot be scientifically certain as to the causes of criminal behavior, tracing the evolution of criminological theories opens the doors to new ideas and perspectives important to those desiring to weigh the pros and cons of the best available information provided by twenty-first century theorists. Some of the theories outlined herein, while discredited by most modern criminologists, have found their way into modern criminal justice systems throughout the world.

Demonological Theory

From the seventeenth to the eighteenth centuries, a loosely organized system of criminological thought gained a great deal of notoriety due in large part to religious and theological explanations for societal behavior considered deviant. The United States was certainly not immune to such mythology, and in fact, the impact of this mode of thinking is present today, though far from predominant.

For an adequate view of the theological connection to criminal behavior in the Western world, we can look back to ancient and medieval times. In ancient Greece, for example, Socrates philosophically sought *the good life.* Aristotle asserted the geocentric theory of the universe, whereby the Earth was the center of life with other heavenly bodies in orbit surrounding the human occupation of this planet. In the world of art, sculptors created magnificent statues to humanlike gods. Music was a popular mode of human entertainment. The literature of the era was replete with the drama of Aeschylus, Sophocles, and Euripides that explored the struggles and relationships of mankind. The chief thread binding philosophical thought during this ancient age was the focus on the plight of humanity. The real Greek mythology stretched way beyond centaurs and gods hurling lightning bolts. The mythology of the people was their belief in the human perspective on things.

The same pattern may be found in the ancient Roman Empire, where *eat, drink, and be merry* was a common belief among the populace. Like ancient Greece,

Rome constructed the symbols of its gods in human form seen in sculptures with lifelike expressions and definitive musculature. Virgil wrote of human adventures, and historians told of the exploits of conquering Roman heroes. This ancient mythology was destined to change in Western Europe.

With the dawn of the Christian era accompanying the birth of Christ, the seeds of changing mythology were planted, and they would grow to affect all aspects of Western human society. For the next thirteen hundred years, the popular focus shifted from humanity to the spiritual God believed by societies to directly influence human affairs. The Christian era leading to what would later be called the *Dark Ages* was the middle period between ancient civilization and the Renaissance in Europe. During this time, there was a distinct universal change in the field of art, for example, where paintings and sculptures no longer displayed human characteristics. Instead theologians, who convinced the populace to construct their societies around religious beliefs, highlighted the glory of the spiritual God. Faces on canvases were now obscure. The eyes of painted subjects were humbly aimed toward the heavens.

Literature glorified God and was didactic only in its spreading of religious doctrine. In music, the artistic mythology shifted to the likes of Gregorian chant, with little focus on humanity. The mindset of Western Europe – the mythology – had been altered drastically.

Although the Renaissance in Western Europe was essentially a *rebirth* of classical thinking from Greece, the heavy religious influence of the Middle Ages left its mark on societies. The impact spread to the New World with the Age of Discovery, and even today religious tenets find their way into modern law.

Seventeenth-century mythologies on criminal justice introduced supernatural explanations for criminal behavior. Human beings declared deviant by local authorities were condemned more for their sins against moral or supernatural authority than for their unethical behavior toward other citizens of the social groups within which they resided. Those local legislators in early America, who retained adherence to the mythology of the Dark Ages despite the intervening Renaissance and Enlightenment periods in Western Europe, viewed human beings as subject to the direct intervention of spiritual forces in the activities of daily living. Criminal laws became reflective of religious doctrine. Degrees of crime mirrored degrees of sin. Satan and other demons were seen as being synonymous with evil. Therefore, someone who violated criminal law also violated spiritual law, because he or she was somehow possessed by the spiritual demons opposing the forces of goodness. Thus, Western Europe experienced the Spanish Inquisition, and in Puritan America, the Salem Witch Trials. Burnings at the stake and tortures for offenses were accepted because criminals were viewed as heretics.

Demonological theories about criminal behavior still exist in the world today. For example, in fundamentalist political theocracies in the Middle East, law reflects religious doctrine. Thus, punishment for behavior considered deviant in those societies is seen as mandated by the wrath of Allah for mala in se activities, rather than mala prohibita legislation by human beings. While the application of such mythology is rare in American thinking today, we do see remnants of the historical impact of religious doctrine on criminal legislation. First Amendment controversies surrounding separation of church and state, abortion issues, political influence by the so-called *religious right,* and arguments surrounding capital punishment are often reflective of religious perspectives.

For most Americans today, demonological theories might appear too far removed from twenty-first century life to command attention, particularly because explanations of deviant behavior as sin or witchcraft have been replaced by psychological, biological, and sociological theories. Nevertheless, such mythology continues to filter through into modern law. As society collectively feels the need to address more universal approaches to crime, crime causation, and crime prevention, new criteria evolve, forming the bases of modern criminological thought.

Classical Theory

The Anglo-American classical theories sprang from the corruption, harsh injustices, tortures, and other cruel punishments of the criminal justice systems in Europe, and in particular, the indiscriminate application of the death penalty for a myriad of social offenses. The Age of Enlightenment that ultimately led to revolutionary thinking in America and France spawned numerous philosophical challenges to demonological-based criminal justice systems. Seventeenth-century writers satirized controlling the behavior of the masses by the powerful as being in violation of human *rights*. This conceptually new mythology spread rapidly as authoritarian governments administered criminal justice with unpredictability.

Enlightenment thinkers stressed the application of science and intellect to social affairs, rather than religion and God's laws. Thinking dominated by the Church in Europe was replaced by scientific approaches to human difficulties. According to Enlightenment mythology, human beings operated in societies of their own free will, not under the direct control of a divine entity. Therefore, as Enlightenment thinkers, social theorists focused on human rights and opposed barbaric treatment of criminals.

One of the most significant of the major theorists opposing the penal policies of the seventeenth century was Englishman Thomas Hobbes (1588-1679. Growing up in the age of Galileo, Hobbes was particularly enthralled with the scientific advances of the late Renaissance era. Like many in his time, he became frustrated with the atrocities of life in Western Europe.

Hobbes reasoned that if it were possible to apply scientific principles to politics, a science of politics based on sound philosophical principles might lead to a peaceful society, free of harsh punishment and abuse.

Hobbes theorized that free people use their senses of reason to create natural laws to which they voluntarily yield for the benefit of all in society. He believed that to build such a peaceful society, forfeiture of merely a minimum amount of human rights is necessary. Thus, by this theory, the creators of law in a political structure are impliedly bound to each other and the government they create by virtue of a social contract. They give up some liberties to the government for the benefit of everyone else in society. In Hobbes' perfect world, free and equal societal members subject themselves to rule by a benevolent sovereign monarch. Of course, application of Hobbes' theory would not eliminate the possibility of rule by a small number of people or a majority, as long as the created form of government has absolute power. However, Hobbes' dependency on science to form natural laws to which human beings would adhere leads him to conclude that freedom in a society of equals is a license to act at the whim of the actor.

Among the leading opponents of criminal policy
during this period was English empiricist philosopher
John Locke (1632-1704). Locke studied at Oxford, where
he became extremely interested in politics and eventually
made substantial contributions to political philosophy. His
Essay Concerning Human Understanding is still
recognized as one of the most significant contributions to
modern philosophical thought in the Western world.

In his *Second Treatise of Government,* Locke sets
forth his political philosophy that profoundly impacted the
criminal policy of his era. Unlike Hobbes, Locke equates
natural law, not with science, but civil law. Based on
traditions of social contract, Locke asserts that liberty
does not mean license. It means the ability to operate
within the government's laws and subject to the
government's punishments for breaking those laws.
Therefore, when Locke speaks of equality, he refers to
equality of rights, not equality of human beings from a
moral or scientific perspective.

To exemplify his theories, Locke explains his
concepts of *reparation and punishment.* Locke's
philosophical world is a natural world of perfect freedom.
This does not mean a license to act as one independently

wishes to act under all circumstances, as would be the case with the application of Hobbes' theory. Societal obligation and natural law dictate that each person must strive not only for self-preservation, but also for the preservation of others. All persons have the right to safeguard their existence and the obligation to safeguard the lives of others. Thus, since rational beings propose the laws to which others are subject, those laws become the natural laws. Executive branches are naturally empowered to enforce those laws that preserve individuals and societies simultaneously. Finally, the judicial branch of government must determine the appropriate punishment to be meted out to citizens who violate the natural laws of society. Therefore, to Locke, even capital punishment is justified, as murderers forfeit their lives by their criminal actions.

Locke argues the basic concepts that make up America's interpretation of democracy. Since the three branches of government share the responsibility of creating and enforcing natural laws to which human beings gravitate, it takes a political society to structure the governmental body entrusted with carrying out the decisions of the majority. The individual power surrendered to the government by the consent of the free people in a society is tantamount to a social contract among all those who voluntarily support the political entity they have created. In doing so, individuals subordinate their rights to the government, no longer retaining individual natural law. The natural law of society is the law created by the governing political body formed by individuals. Locke's idea of surrendering rights to the political society through a social contract does not leave citizens devoid of rights. Members of society can always change the legislative, executive, or judicial branches of government to suit their collective needs. However, individuals would forever lose the right to personally legislate, to carry out the law, and to mete out punishment.

In France, Jean-Jacques Rousseau (1712-1778) led the fight for the reformation of the system of punishment that was deemed a violation of human rights. In the development of his theories, he disputed the works of Hobbes and Locke, and had a profound influence on the later work of Immanuel Kant and Karl Marx.

Rousseau's concept of social contract is contained in his famous *Discourse on Inequality.* Like Hobbes and Locke, Rousseau interprets natural law as man-made law. However, he presents the negative side of societal structure. Rousseau sees the formation of civil societies as human regression causing misery and inequality through never-ending competition among the populace in a complex society. Socialization, therefore, creates inequality, especially by virtue of the manner in which labor is divided among citizens, creating further inequities. According to Rousseau, division of labor in society causes the less advantaged to help the more advantaged, leading to greater disadvantage among the poor. Thus, society exacerbates inequality.

To overcome the complexities of large, inequitable social groups humans call societies, Rousseau interprets the implied social contract between the individual and the community quite differently than Hobbes and Locke. Whereas Hobbes and Locke propose the relinquishment of minimal rights to the majority represented by the governing body, Rousseau advocates the relinquishment of all rights, equalizing all members of society, thereby eliminating the built-in competition of socialization.

Rousseau's conception of freedom is moral freedom. He suggests that the equalization process leads to the ethical right to work for the benefit of the greater whole. Thus, under this theory, those who have alienated their individual rights to the greater whole have submitted to the will of the greater whole. This greater will is indivisible. Consequently, all laws are applied equally. For example, suppose the general will of society mandates capital punishment for murder. This would mean that murderers have by virtue of their relinquishment of all rights to society consented to capital punishment for their crimes. Their individual preferences do not count because they have been alienated to society. Likewise, society cannot deal with murderers on an individual basis, because the same general will applies to all members of society. Therefore, the laws apply equally to everyone.

Rousseau takes his vision of social contract one step further than Hobbes and Locke. Both Hobbes and Locke make the assumption that in the process of relinquishing some rights for the betterment of the whole equitable laws are formed by the will of the people. Rousseau believes the masses of people incapable of understanding the complexities of law sufficiently to develop equitable legislation. The consent of the governed is not informed consent. His preference is the elite, educated benevolent legislator who will determine the true interests of the governed. This theory greatly influenced later philosophical and political thought, preparing fertile ground for the seeds of Marxism.

The outgrowth of the philosophical perspectives of Hobbes, Locke, and Rousseau was classical theory. Indeed, classical theory was the product of Enlightenment philosophy. Their collective philosophical concepts helped to form the underlying motivations for revolution on two continents. Furthermore, portions of the American Constitution, such as the Eighth Amendment prohibition against cruel and unusual punishment, can be directly linked to this era.

Of course, Hobbes, Locke, and Rousseau were primarily philosophers, sociologists, and political critics. While their theories are not founded in criminology, they do form the building blocks of thoughts on crime causation and crime solutions. One of the chief proponents of the classical school of criminological thought was Italian criminologist Cesare Beccaria (1738-

1794), whose essay entitled *On Crimes and Punishments* helped to shift the mythology of Europe and America toward the concept of *just* punishment:

> In order for punishment not to be [...] an act of violence of one or many against a private citizen, it must be essentially public, prompt, necessary, the least possible in the given circumstances, proportionate to the crimes, dictated by the laws. (Beccaria 99)

His writings focused on two central positions: the philosophy of utilitarianism, the greatest good for the greatest number of people, and the concept of the social contract, based on Hobbes' theories, whereby citizens impliedly sacrifice a minimum amount of personal rights for the betterment of society as a whole. Beccaria relied on these philosophical principles in asserting his view of the underlying purposes of punishment for unacceptable societal behavior. To Beccaria, revenge had no place in punitive measures taken by societies. He remained steadfast in his belief that improvement of society's crime problems mandated deterrence as a weapon against deviant behavior. In Beccaria's view, by connecting appropriate punishments to specific crimes, those inclined to deviate from societal norms would be deterred from such acts.

Beccaria was a devout student of the Enlightenment period in eighteenth-century France. In both Europe and the American colonies, the Enlightenment described a feeling of emergence from ignorance, theological rule, and Church authority in secular matters, and movement toward reason and respect for humanity not previously enjoyed. The Enlightenment defined an *attitude* of change and re-evaluation of values, including moral values, designed to improve the quality of life shared by the populace. Education was suggested as a viable tool to improve living conditions. Modern liberalism is modeled in great part on Enlightenment principles. By studying the writings of Voltaire, Montesquieu, Hobbes, Hume, and Rousseau, Beccaria was able to formulate a deep personal sense of the lack of ethics surrounding the application of punishment methodologies such as torture and death techniques aimed at achieving justice. His work became enormously popular among the middle and lower classes throughout Europe, eventually impacting upon the changes to penal codes previously enacted. His writings held particular significance for pre-revolutionary American and French citizens.

Beccaria was outraged by the arbitrariness of the application of punishment by government authority. He saw little value in a system utilizing torture to extract confessions and cruel beatings for a wide range of offenses, so wide that criminals were unable to decipher the connection between the crime and the punishment. For example, if insulting a government official carried the same penalty as murder, the accused would hardly be deterred from crime as it would be impossible to determine what offenses were punishable by specific penalties. From his vantage point, unjust laws served to criminalize non-deviant behavior. In a nutshell, his philosophy, giving rise to classical theory, was to *let the punishment fit the crime.* The contemporary concept of mandatory punishment is a remnant of this theory.

Beccaria's philosophical position should not be interpreted as softness on crime. Quite the contrary, he understood that the unwritten social contract he promoted could not in and of itself prevent or deal with social crime. While he stressed crime prevention, he urged effective crime deterrence through appropriate punishment.

Principles of *general* and *specific* deterrence adopted by modern American lawmakers and upheld by U.S. courts in the twenty-first century find their direct roots in Beccaria's theories, although he provided little scientific bases for his conclusions. General deterrence is aimed at establishing punishment examples for societal members to see for the purpose of allowing them to think twice about the commission of criminal acts. In theory, the general population is dissuaded by this method. Specific deterrence, on the other hand, is aimed at the individual criminal to prevent recidivism or repeat offending. By sentencing the criminal actor to a fitting punishment, he or she, theoretically, would be dissuaded from future criminal behavior. Therefore, Beccaria's theories did not suggest making punishments lighter, but simply more proportionately appropriate to the crime committed.

Beccaria's famous work *On Crimes and Punishments* is considered by criminologists to be one of the first written expressions of opposition to the concept

of capital punishment. Beccaria preferred Hobbes'
theories concerning the minimal relinquishment of
individual rights in favor of the public good over Locke's
theories concerning forfeiture of life for serious crimes.
Thus, in his interpretation of Hobbes' philosophy,
Beccaria asserted that people do not deliver their lives to
the public welfare, but reserve their collective right to
life, thereby preventing societies from ethically enforcing
death penalties. He further attacked capital punishment
on the grounds of its uselessness for societies, since it
does not deter crime. In his view, altering the mythology
of a society is a far more effective deterrent to deviant
behavior than the death of a few individuals. He believed
long-term imprisonment provides more of a horrible
picture to members of societies than the prospect of
death.

Among the best of Beccaria's advanced solutions
to crime problems was the suggestion of education as a
combatant methodology. Education as a sword in the
fight against crime is still highly touted today.

The classical school viewed deviant behavior as
being motivated by *hedonism*. Proponents reasoned,
based on psychological theories, that human beings were

motivated by one of two factors: pleasure or pain.
Humans, they asserted, act for their own hedonistic
enjoyment, or conversely, do not act out of fear of pain.
Thus, they concluded, criminals operate in a deviant
manner by their own *free will.* This being understood, it
became logical to exact punishment according to the
severity of the criminal behavior because the offender
had intentionally acted in a manner contrary to collective
societal controls. The control over the criminal element in
society would be more effective if the thrill of violating
criminal laws did not outweigh the pain of punishment
for such offenses.

Classical theory had a profound impact upon
Western criminal justice systems. It was based on the
democratic principle of law as a reflection of all segments
of society. The Eighth Amendment prohibition in the U.S.
Constitution against cruel and unusual punishment is a
direct outgrowth of Beccaria's philosophy that became
American mythology. Additionally, Beccaria specifically
argued the contemporary concept of *determinate
sentencing,* whereby legislators, who simultaneously
provide limited judicial discretion in the adjustment of
prescribed punishments, establish sentences. Likewise

modern *mandatory sentencing*, effectively eliminating judicial discretion in the punishment process, is also based on Beccaria's mythology of crime prevention. These theories were not and are not without critics since they treat all criminal actors without regard to extenuating circumstances. Factors such as age, mental capacity, number of offenses, and mitigating circumstances are not considered, primarily because social contract assumes societal consensus.

Utilitarianism is another classical school of philosophical thought that had a profound impact upon nineteenth-century criminological theory. Utilitarianism promotes the construction of a societal mindset whereby ethical behavior is determined by actions that result in the greatest amount of good to the greatest number of people. The leading advocate of utilitarianism, who derived many of his theories from the work of Beccaria, was Jeremy Bentham (1748-1832).

Bentham spent most of his life studying and writing about the reform of social institutions. As a philosopher with an emphasis on ethics, he advanced several theories pertaining to politics, the most significant of which was demonstrated in *Introduction to the*

Principles of Morals and Legislation. It is in this work that Bentham expressed his now famous *greatest happiness* principle. By doing so, he instantly became an original proponent of utilitarianism.

As in Beccaria's case, Enlightenment thinkers such as Voltaire, Hume, and Locke heavily influenced Bentham's philosophy. Furthermore, he adopted Beccaria's theories of hedonism to explain the psychological motivations of the criminal elements in society. Developing the theory of psychological egoism, Bentham asserted that human beings are self-centered by nature. However, to effectuate the best possible societal scenario of harmony, human beings should act ethically, or in other words, only in a manner productive of the greatest amount of societal happiness. He reasoned it was the primary responsibility of lawmakers to create statutory schemes that tended to join diverse social groups with varied personal interests in harmony.

In applying his utilitarian theories to societies, Bentham stressed the equality of *value* shared by human beings. Everyone was assessed the same value in society, no one person being more important than any other member. Thus, Bentham did not express the concept of freedom in positive terms, but negative ones. He considered liberty to constitute the *absence of restraint.* He visualized freedom only in the context of society, not as a fundamental human right. Therefore, freedom was consistent with utilitarianism since it provided the greatest amount of pleasure to the most people in a society.

Bentham rejected the concept of social contract. Instead, he preferred the notion that rights are created legally, not fundamentally, unless they are fundamental to the happiness of the greatest number of people. This theory is still advanced in the formulation of modern American law, where legislatures seek to provide for the common good.

Neoclassical Theory

The neoclassical schools of thought that emerged in the late nineteenth century ultimately replaced many of Bentham's theories. Neoclassical thinkers asserted the need to reform the classical school of thought, especially in the areas of inflexible punishments. Neoclassical criminologists sought to introduce for consideration collateral factors that might have impacted criminal acts. Fixed punishments for particular crimes were rejected in favor of modifications of sentences after consideration of intelligence quotients, ages, emotional factors, heredity factors, motivations, and incidents of prior criminal activity among the convicted. Neoclassical theory admits environmental, psychological, and other mitigating or extenuating circumstances as modifying conditions to the classical theory. Thus, proponents urged special treatment for juveniles, insane persons, and those motivated by special circumstances to commit crime. *Indeterminate Sentencing,* whereby courts are provided by legislators with wide ranges of discretionary punishments and *Rehabilitation,* which is designed to re-introduce criminals into society as productive members, are outgrowths of neoclassical theory.

Positivist Theory

Philosophical theorists like Rene Descartes, Baruch Spinoza, and Gottfried Leibniz proposed rationalist theories based upon the concept of innate human understanding of things. Contrarily, empiricist thinkers like George Berkeley, David Hume, and John Locke asserted the need to learn through the senses and experiences. Emanating from empirical theories, nineteenth-century criminological approaches evolved into a major ideology known as *positivism*, pursuant to which the two major concerns with respect to the reorganization of social life are individuals and their social conduct.

Positivist theory deals with the application of scientific principles to organize a given society into a controlled social life for the good of all its citizens. As empirical theory and scientific experimentation grew in popularity, scientists suggested the possibility that humans evolved at different levels. Thus, as science moved away from religious belief and free will was questioned as a causal factor in human behavior, social and biological factors determining human behavior were advanced.

Positivist thinking is diametrically opposed to classical thinking. For positivists, the concept of free will was replaced by *determinism*. Determinist thinking stresses crime prevention rather than crime punishment based on the notion that punishing people for behavior beyond their control is unethical. Sociological attempts to mitigate the circumstances causing activities considered deviant comprise the preferred approach by determinists.

In the seventeenth century, noted rationalist philosopher Benedict de Spinoza (1632-1677) rejected the notion of free will in criminal actions. He asserted other factors like inherited characteristics and external environmental stimuli render one's actions pre-determined. Thus, according to Spinoza, it would be folly to punish someone for actions over which he or she had no control.

One of the most popular applications of determinist philosophy to criminology lies in the very underlying principle of American law that dictates crime as a component of two separate factors. To commit an offense deemed criminal, a perpetrator's act must include *actus reus,* the criminal act itself, and *mens rea,* the criminal intent. Thus, the voluntary commission of a crime is essential to punishment for the action. Actions beyond the actor's control, or determined acts, are not criminal. This is why American jurisprudence allows for exceptions to criminal punishment for acts committed by minors, the mentally insane, and involuntarily intoxicated individuals.

Positivism is of significance to modern sociologists and criminologists because it is the mythology that planted the seeds to what was to become the doctrine of socialism. Auguste Comte (1798-1857) was a French positivist who theorized on political reconstruction of the social order prevalent in many nineteenth-century societies by the implementation of scientific processes that evolve naturally within political entities. His sociological approach to politics was diametrically opposed to the principles of democracy, especially American style democracy. Human problems, according to Comte, could be resolved more efficiently in societies where elite classes apply scientific principles to social order in hopes of improving the overall human condition. While Comte's philosophical expressions of socialist thinking were not quite identical to the ultimate political mythology of twentieth-century socialism, his contribution to the historical development of this ideology bears a direct relationship to the government treatment of nonconformists studied by modern criminologists.

Comte rejected the concept of free will. He believed governments should be reorganized so as to provide the most intellectual people with the social control over the uneducated masses. While the scientific minds in society could move progress along, input by the lower classes who knew little about the operations of nineteenth-century political and economic social institutions would send society in a negative direction. In Comte's view, the scientific *intelligencia* ruled naturally, while those with lower social status should resign themselves to being ruled.

Modern socialism is an outgrowth of the substandard working conditions and poor economic prospects associated with the industrial revolution. Even today, proponents of socialism assert the inequity of leaving one's individual circumstances in society to chance or individual effort. For example, one citizen might inherit a fortune, another might acquire wealth through extra effort or hard work, and another might remain less economically fortunate. Socialists argue in favor of minimum wages and minimum standards of working conditions.

The nature of socialist philosophy lends itself to the requirement that property and wealth in society be owned by the state and redistributed through some peaceful political mechanism or process. Thus, the nationalization of societal organizations is mandatory. Ultimately, carrying this ideology to its logical conclusion, societal cooperation would exist in a classless community.

Socialist theory as an outgrowth of positivist theory is of particular significance to modern criminologists who suggest crime is a social illness, rather than a result of voluntary actions by individuals. Positivism, in a nutshell, fostered the concept of *let the punishment fit the criminal.* Criminals were viewed as sick, and therefore, the focus was on the criminal, not the crime. Positivists believed criminals should be *treated* for their crimes, not punished. This perspective is still followed by many contemporary criminologists.

Psychological Theory

Psychological theories are frequently categorized collectively as psychological positivism. Many of these theories, especially the psychoanalytic ones, are derivatives of the lifetime work of Sigmund Freud (1859-1939), who did not study criminality per se. Nevertheless, Freud's theories on human behavior and psychosexual development led to a greater understanding of the motivations of psychopaths, sociopaths, and other deviant personalities. From Freud's perspective, antisocial personalities were considered symptomatic, and, therefore, could be treated for deeply rooted problems through psychotherapy.

Another influential psychological theory that attracted much attention in the early part of the twentieth century dealt with the relationship between low intelligence quotients and incidents of criminal behavior. Henry Goddard (1866-1957) promoted this nexus in his work *Feeblemindedness: Its Causes and Consequences.* While Goddard's scientific data was far from complete, later criminologists acknowledged the role of intelligence in many instances of criminal behavior, but only on an individual basis. At the very least, intelligence was thought to be as good a predictor of delinquent behavior as race, poverty, or social class. However, no definitive conclusions could be reached to accurately suggest criminals possess less intelligence than non-criminals.

In his famous treatise *Escape from Freedom,* Erich Fromm (1900-1980) asserted a strong connection between psychological and sociological factors emanating from a human need to belong that could lead to criminality. Fromm suggested that psychological processes motivating individuals impact social process directly in the same manner social cultures impact and mold individuals directly. In other words, psychological components of individuals help to form societies, while societal cultures in turn help to pattern behavioral tendencies of individuals in a societal group. As a result, according to Fromm, people isolated and powerless in society continually seek greater levels of freedom and independence. Once the desired level of freedom is attained, humans become more independent, which leads to further isolation. As the cycle continues, humans surrender a certain degree of freedom to controlling societal groups of which they become a very small part. The controlling group to which they have imparted their independence then cares for its citizens who have relinquished the freedom they originally sought to attain.

In *Escape from Freedom,* Fromm examines the emergence of individuals from birth and relates the individual experience to the historical and social development of humankind. The growth process takes humans from the *oneness* with nature they share at the beginning of life to the separation from others they achieve on maturity. He calls the maturation process the emergence of *individuation.* When children are born, they emerge as separate biological entities to find themselves in total dependence upon their mothers. From the moment of birth, children strive for separation from the controlling parent until they are able to cut the primary ties of the symbolic umbilical cord as they achieve independence. Yet, mothers remain part of the lives of their children. Human beings remain connected to the universe, though the control asserted over them is quite different from the dependency at birth. The stronger the growth process and the stronger the sense of self becomes, the more humans experience *aloneness.* As individuals become more powerful, they become more alone and increasingly anxious, ultimately developing a stronger sense of powerlessness. This spawns overwhelming impulses to give up freedom and individuality to overcome powerlessness and aloneness.

Examining criminality from Fromm's perspective, one can readily see that the child's impossible task of returning to the mother's womb reflects a societal citizen's inability to reverse the individuation process. The result of man's frustration in his assumption of submissive characteristics in society is insecurity, which often generates hostility and rebellion. But according to Fromm, this need not occur because just as independent children are bound to their mothers in a different way than they experienced during their growing years, societal members might retain a high degree of independence while submitting to societal relationships. Freedom takes on a different meaning for the individual in society than its connotation during the individuation process. Human behavior is no longer classified as *freedom to* operate separately from submission to the mother figure, but *freedom from* the impulses to submit to controlling entities. In other words, human beings have choices.

Fromm's psychological theories tend to explain human tendencies to act from instinct, or the biological human weaknesses that seep into cultural conditions. As human dependency, helplessness, or determined behavior grows, people search for mechanisms of escape from societal submissions. Ironically, there is conflict, because growing independence breeds insecurity, separation, uncertainty, and powerlessness compelling human beings to enter into relationships with other societal members and institutions – a kind of submission. Modern capitalism would appear to be a cultural institution required to connect individuals to the greater whole and each other, while simultaneously allowing for individuation. The essential conclusion derived from Fromm's theories is that freedom comes with responsibility. The alternative is authoritarian control. The application to criminological thought is the need for individual conformity to society to avoid unwanted control and resultant loss of individual freedom.

Economic Theory

Based largely upon the theories of philosopher Hegel, Karl Marx (1818-1883), primarily in *Das Capital* and his co-authored *Communist Manifesto,* adopted the *dialectic* concept, whereby society evolves in a manner similar to human evolution. Marx reasoned that constant conflicts between theses and antitheses ultimately produce *syntheses.* According to this theory, societies adopt certain propositions that are subsequently challenged by members in that society who propose alternate propositions. Eventually, the two conflicting theses produce a new proposition synthesizing into a third proposition. Marx claimed the cycle continues in all societies. Applying Marx's evolutionary synthesis concept to societal economics ultimately results in *communism.* Today, we recognize the failure of world communism, but the development of the theory has greatly impacted modern criminological theories that are sociologically grounded.

Most early economic criminological theories stem from Marx, despite the fact that he never directly applied his theoretical findings to crime. Criminologists did note, however, the obvious implications from Marxian deterministic economic philosophy that capitalism creates economic inequality. Since it is widely believed economic disparity is a leading factor in criminal behavior, the relationship between Marxist doctrine and crime is a natural one. Thus, early economic theories focused not on the individual criminal, but on the underlying deficient society in which the criminal activity was taking place.

Dutch philosopher Willem Bonger (1876-1940) adopts Marxist theory in developing his criminological conclusions as to crime causation and prevention. In his most influential work, *Criminality and Economic Conditions,* Bonger asserts the very purpose of criminal law to be the protection of property rights of the upper economic classes. Bonger claims capitalism promotes and encourages selfishness in societies, along with competition for basic human needs.

Bonger, following Marx, does not believe in *consensus* in a capitalist society. He sees criminal law as a method of serving ruling class interests, rather than a mechanism for controlling deviant behavior. He points to crimes committed by the rich that remain un-prosecuted. The result of self-serving criminal laws aimed at protecting property rights is, in Bonger's view, a direct cause of poverty, which ultimately spawns crime.

Interestingly, the theories of Marx and Bonger pre-date the application of socialism and communism to twentieth-century world societies. Thus, early economic theory was just that – theory. Later, however, Radical Marxist criminologists revisited criminological economic theory, much of which is still followed worldwide and studied seriously in modern American culture. In the criminal justice system, the relationship between economic depravity and criminal behavior might require further clarity, but, as an often predominant factor in deviant behavior, must be examined more closely by modern criminologists bent on solutions.

Ecological Theory

Ecological schools of criminological thought, also known as geographical theories of criminology, are grounded in several sciences. Most often, they blend biology, the study of organisms, with ecology, the study of the environment. Ecological criminologists search for the causes of crime in the interrelationships among human beings as biological organisms and their physical environments.

Probably the first major criminological work in this field was that of A.M. Guerry (1802-1866) of France. Guerry took a scientific approach to criminology by studying maps, charts, and statistical data in search of commonalities of environmental factors among those who had committed crimes.

Similarly, the first recognized scientific criminologist was Lambert Adolphe Jacques Quetelet (1786-1874) of Belgium. Quetelet's primary purpose in pursuing ecological theories was an attempt to discredit the classical theorists. To accomplish his goal, he completed extensive studies in the disciplines of psychology and sociology in order to monitor the impact of factors other than free will on the criminal element in society.

In his famous *Treatise on Man and the Development of His Faculties,* he asserts the strong influence of sociological, economic, gender, and age factors on crime. "Society carries within itself [...] the seeds of all the crimes which are going to be committed, together with the facilities necessary for their development (Quetelet 308). He indicated his studies involving *thermic law* reveal that, especially among juveniles, property crimes appear to be more prevalent in colder climates and during winter seasons. Conversely, violent crimes increase in warmer climates and during summer seasons. Additionally, Quetelet is among the first criminologists to suggest the concept of *relative deprivation,* whereby the gap between one's status and the expectation of success might be linked to crime causation. This important criminological concept is developed more completely by Durkheim, and later Merton in his famous anomie theory.

Other ecological theories appear to have some relevance to crime causation, but much of the supporting scientific data is questionable or incomplete. For example, the phases of the moon affect tides, atmospheric pressure, and animal behavior. Ecological criminologists assert the same effect upon human behavior.

French philosopher Baron de Montesquieu (1689-1755) theorized a connection between climate and crime. His studies tended to reveal a statistical link between warmer climates and violent crimes and colder climates and property crimes. Montesquieu asserted that excessive alcohol consumption increases the farther away human beings get from the equator, whereas violent criminality increases nearer to the equator. The difficulty with such theory is the apparent overlooking of relevant cultural phenomena during statistical and scientific studies. For example, sociological concepts such as the increased interaction among human beings during warmer months of the year might explain the increase in violence during those same time periods.

Biological Theory

In the nineteenth century, Charles Darwin ((1809-1882) authored his famous work *On the Origin of Species by Means of Natural Selection.* Having nothing at all to do with criminological findings, Darwin's studies suggested evolution as a factor altering living species over long periods of time. Darwin theorized that all species, including *homo sapiens,* produce offspring that do not survive because they do not possess the most favorable characteristics suited for survival. Nature *selects* the most capable species with the most favorable qualities for survival. Thus, as future generations of survivors continually reproduce, the natural selection process continues, selecting the strongest members with the best chances to survive. Darwin's theories had an enormous impact upon criminological theory.

Criminologists like Gall and Lombroso studied Darwinian Theory in the formation of their assertions concerning the link between crime and biological evolution.

Beginning with the eighteenth century, criminologists drifted away from demonological, supernatural, and theological explanations of the causes of crime in favor of a more scientific approach. This approach generally assumed deviants and criminals to differ physiologically from conforming members of society. Among the first theorists to assert a new perspective was German scientist Franz Joseph Gall (1758-1828). Gall studied the structural makeup of the human skull to determine a possible connection between the physical configuration of the skull and a human propensity toward criminal behavior. He was one of the first scientists to attempt to localize certain mental functions of the human brain. By doing so, he hoped to identify personality types through a process called *cranioscopy,* later referred to as *phrenology.* In his famous work, *The Anatomy and Physiology of the Nervous System in General, and of the Brain in Particular,* Gall outlined his theories in a manner easily understood by early nineteenth-century societies. Consistent with the philosophical doctrines of the rationalists, Gall's theories began with the underlying premise that human beings have innate intelligence. He extended his theories, however, by concluding that the manifestation of human intellectual faculties largely depends on the manner in which the brain is organized internally. Gall asserted that the human brain is comprised of several sections or components called *organs.* These organs develop differently in each person. The extent of development or growth of the interior sections of the brain is reflected in the outward configuration of the cranium. Therefore, by studying the shape of the skull, one might identify physical similarities among criminals that reflect commonalities in deviant personalities.

While Gall's theories were immensely popular during the nineteenth century, they were ultimately rejected as scientifically unsound. The popularity of phrenology was due in part to acceptance by imperialist English ruling classes attempting to prove their subjects (particularly Irish and American colonists) were inferior human beings. In the twentieth century, many of Gall's conclusions were shown to have scientific accuracy, but the methodology used to draw theories on cerebral localization was highly inaccurate. Nevertheless, Gall's work was expanded upon by later criminologists such as Cesare Lombroso, who in his book entitled *Criminal Anthropology* associated skull and facial features with criminal types, adding further emphasis on a scientific approach to the study of crime to the developing discipline of criminology.

Italian criminologist Cesare Lombroso (1835-1909) advanced the theories propounded by Franz Joseph Gall. Drawing upon Darwin's theories of evolution and natural selection, Lombroso focused on heredity and the common traits of people prone to commit crimes and participate in deviant acts. In his scientific experiments, he examined and measured the skulls of modern humans, prehistoric humans, and apes to assess similarities and differences. His conclusions advanced a theory know as *atavism,* by which criminals are deemed to be atavistic, or savage throwbacks to early man. Early humans possessed certain qualities, characteristics, and traits that better enabled them to hunt, kill, and otherwise survive in uncivilized societal groups. Those more likely to commit violent criminal offenses in modern societies were evolutionary primitives. In his influential study entitled *Criminal Man,* Lombroso linked subcultural realities such as tattooing to atavistic tendencies. These conclusions helped to link criminal behavior to biological factors among the scientific communities of the nineteenth century. The notion of humans being *born criminal* was revolutionary. Eventually, Lombroso did concede the significant presence of sociological factors in the development of deviant personalities. Nevertheless, in his application of his theories to criminological studies, he provided the building blocks for future theorists – many of whom developed lasting theories while simply attempting to dispute Lombroso.

Lombroso is sometimes (although erroneously) referred to as the father of modern criminology largely because his popular theories promoted scientific credibility in crime studies. His theories were not rejected until the twentieth century. Modern criminologists and sociologists continue to argue, however, humane governments must not punish human beings biologically incapable of acceptable social behavior.

Charles Goring (1870-1919) did much to discredit the findings of Cesare Lombroso. The British criminologist explored the concept of the *criminal type,* largely by examining prison inmates in search of commonalities. While Goring's findings revealed no such connection among those labeled deviant by society, later twentieth-century studies do confirm possible links between certain brain abnormalities and tendencies toward criminality.

Goring published *The English Convict* in 1913. This work revealed his extensive studies of thousands of criminal and non-criminal subjects for comparison. His findings tended to dispute Lombroso's conclusions as to any commonality of physical characteristics among the criminal elements in society, but Goring did conclude some recognizable mental deficiencies among deviant personalities. At the time, Goring's theories were highly touted in the United States, until the adoption of standards for military testing for citizens conscripted into World War I were developed based on his findings. Applying Goring's methodology, one-third of those tested fell into the category of *feeblemindedness* with propensities toward criminal behavior. The required modification of standards sufficient to man American military forces spelled doom for Goring's biological theories. Despite this historical reality, modern criminologists using technologically advanced methods are currently revisiting the issue of identification of the *criminal personality* largely based on Goring's theories and subsequent studies.

Harvard anthropologist and Lombrosian Earnest Hooton (1887-1954) wrote *Crime and the Man* in 1939, which study purported to focus on the organic inferiority of criminals. Hooton wildly suggested extermination of the physically and mentally unsound, or at the very least, the total isolation and segregation of the criminal element from the rest of society. Coming from a professor at Harvard University in the United States, Hooton's theories created quite a controversy, since the year of the release of his study coincided with the atrocities of Nazi Germany.

Sheldon Glueck (1896-1980) and Eleanor Glueck (1898-1972) approached the study of criminology from the biological perspective through their research on juvenile delinquency. The Gluecks focused on the possible relationship between body types and criminal behavior patterns. Gathering their material from a wide variety of sources, these researchers examined age, gender, race, ethnicity, and economic status. Nevertheless, their studies have been widely criticized as being too vague, resulting in no definitive conclusions that could be accurately applied to juveniles. They were able, however, to expose the need to consider environmental factors in the study of crime causation.

Lesson Two: Modern Sociological Theories

Virtually all the modern criminological theories are sociological in nature. Twenty-first century criminologists take a multidisciplinary approach to the study of crime causation with an eye toward offering potential societal improvements that might tend to lessen problematic human activity. For example, as socialism became a more viable theory in the twentieth century, social-minded criminologists began to explore possible links between poverty and criminal activity. Especially in the area of non-violent offenses, studies connected incidents of property, theft, and burglary crimes to those less advantaged. Theorists asserted positions suggesting those unable to support themselves adequately through mainstream means of employment were actually *driven* to crime by society. Environmental factors, unemployment, overcrowded or substandard living conditions, lack of recreational outlets, inadequate sanitation, and other social phenomena were blamed for widespread feelings of hopelessness among the poor in American society. Sociologists concluded that criminal activity might be a viable alternative to conformity among the poverty-stricken. From a sociological perspective, according to theories previously advanced, segments of American society view crime as a means to attain success among those economically deprived. Among the poor, especially the young, crime figures appear heroic, becoming models of achievement to emulate.

Much of the emphasis in the twentieth century remained on the psychological causations for criminal behavior. The mentally challenged, the emotionally challenged, and the psychotic were objects of studies that revealed tendencies in these groups toward deviant behavior.

One of the primary reasons contemporary criminologists have rejected the early criminological theories discussed previously has more to do with approach than lack of merit. While many theories have been scientifically discredited, others remain viable and valuable. Nevertheless, the modern perspective relies on a more multidisciplinary approach to crime causation and potential crime solutions. In effect, modern theorists assert no single cause of criminal behavior. While individual theories might have merit, and specific studies might be of value to future criminologists, no one theory explains all facets of deviant behavior. The favored modern approach is to take various vantage points into consideration when formulating solutions to the crime problem. Thus, a synthesis of possible causations (discussed more thoroughly in the Conclusion) results in potential solutions to the crime problem in the United States based upon psychiatric, psychological, biological, sociological, cultural, economic, philosophical, and historical considerations. It is important to note, however, that like early classical, psychological, and biological theories of criminology, sociological theories focus on the criminal actor as the unit of analysis, rather than the crime itself.

One of the most influential figures to impact modern criminological attitudes was French social theorist, Emile Durkheim (1858-1917). He believed in the application of scientific methodology to the study of societies, in part to determine the causes of social instability. Durkheim theorized that societal groups have identities that stretch far beyond the sum total of the characteristics of the individual human beings that comprise the group. He studied societal value systems such as religion and morality to better assess the ties among societal groups and their memberships. To Durkheim, frustration, dissatisfaction, and even crime result from the dissipation of societal values.

From a sociological perspective, Durkheim promoted the theory of *functionalism* or the *consensus theory* of sociology. According to this view, the preferable society operates in harmony, all social groups cooperating with one another. Beyond simple cooperative efforts, functionalists believe viable social systems thrive because each segment of society provides specific contributions to the whole. Thus, even crime is a *necessary* element of the whole. This is in contrast to the *conflict theory* of sociology, which projects continual conflicts among the various groups in society. Since Durkheim believed in the necessity of controlling social crises, he looked to ideologies that could lead to new widespread mythologies aimed at the survival of societies as a whole. Functionalism fit the bill perfectly since the theory does not espouse crime prevention, only crime containment within acceptable societal limits.

By examining society as a unified organism analogous to the human body, Durkheim was able to explore ways to maintain social order. Just like healthy organs are essential to the health of the human body as a whole, healthy value systems that impose norms upon its members are also essential to thriving societies. Thus, functionalism looks at diverse parts of society to determine common values that promote social order.

As a result of Durkheim's acceptance of functionalist theory, he introduced his concept of *anomie*, or a state of *normlessness* in society. In his book entitled *The Division of Labor in Society*, he suggested that social rules that people voluntarily adhere to often break down. The philosophical ethics of groups in communities or the way people expect to treat each other and be treated by each other become unclear, causing some to become confused about expectations of behavior. Durkheim asserted that this moral breakdown leads to deviant behavior and crime. When societies grow, becoming more complex, people lose the social bonds that connect them with each other. Thus, the relationship among members of the social community becomes more impersonal and norms no longer control their activities. Durkheim used the term anomie to refer to such a breakdown of societal values. When this occurs, people are no longer able to feel comfortable with their respective places in society because they have no definitive rules for guiding their behavior. As societal conditions change in such an atmosphere, tension results leading to deviant behavior. In other words, when the social system of norms breaks down, deviant behavior thrives. Durkheim claimed this happens most often as work conditions change substantially. The solution advanced was to create complex divisions of labor in society, making workers realize their dependency upon one another. Thus, he concluded, compassion for humanity develops preventing deviant behavior.

Durkheim's contributions stress that social facts rather than moral rules control social conduct. People respond to these social phenomena more positively than they do to the imposition of controls by governments.

Anomie Theory

Building upon Durkheim's concept of anomie, sociologist Robert K. Merton (1910-2003) asserted his *strain* theory, establishing a strong relationship between the structure of a society and the cultural goals maintained in that society. According to Merton, the existing culture in the United States assumes all societal members share the common goal of attainment of wealth. Many citizens agree that it appears the *American Dream* does not include economic return. Americans seek comfortable living accommodations, adequate income to support families, luxuries not enjoyed in other countries, education, happiness, and a countless number of material items many of us deem necessities of life. Nevertheless, the legitimate means to achieve these goals are not always provided to or accessible by some segments of society. Therefore, certain social classes, most likely the lower economic classes, fall into the status of anomie. When the gap between the desired cultural goals and any reasonable expectation of achieving those goals through legitimate means becomes too wide, individuals adapt in ways that lead to criminal activity.

As stated above, anomie is a state in which clear-cut norms that guide human conduct appear to be absent. When the norms, rules, standards, and expectations regarding behavior usually shared in society are lacking for individuals, they tend to gravitate toward antisocial behavior. Building upon Merton's theory, Richard Cloward (1926-2001) and Lloyd Ohlin (1918-2008) published their *differential opportunity* theory in 1960 aimed at juvenile gang activity. Cloward and Ohlin theorized about the formation of subcultures as adaptations to anomic situations. They asserted that lower class youth deprived of legitimate opportunities to succeed in their communities turn to illegitimate opportunities provided by subcultures like gangs, which rely on deviant behavioral patterns to realize their aspirations.

Social Process Theory

Social Process theories emanate from the University of Chicago, which provided America's first academic program in sociology in 1892. This line of philosophical thought became known as the *Chicago School* and proved significant in the development of criminological theory in the twentieth century.

The basic premise of social process theorists is the notion that crime is due more to social disorganization than to abnormal individuals participating in deviant behavior. This thinking evolved into a series of *learning theories.* The approach began with an assumption that the activation of psychological characteristics influencing human aggression depends largely on a learning process. Thus, deviant behavior and the nature of the deviant behavior are within the control of the criminal. Social learning determines whether the individual will display the aggressive behavior he or she learns.

Twentieth-century criminologist Edwin Sutherland (1883-1950) proposed one of the most popular and influential learning theories, much of which still impacts criminological thinking in 2019. In what he labeled the *differential association* theory, Sutherland characterized criminality as a learned, sub-cultural transmission of criminal values. He concluded excess social contacts that advocate criminal behavior pre-dispose individuals toward criminality. In other words, when individuals maintain regular social contacts with people whose attitudes favor criminality, they learn to accept criminal values as the norm. For example, criminological studies reveal the focus of many lower class cultures on trouble, machismo, the excitement of flirtation with danger, and the process of becoming streetwise. For many such individuals, the future is simply a matter of fate or luck. Thus, they learn their values from those sharing similar attitudes, forming sub-cultures inclined toward deviant criminal behavior.

Social Control Theory

Social Control theories deal with the manner by which control is exercised over citizens. Those subscribing to such theories assert that the methods of social control established in a civilized society determine whether people will either conform or become deviant. Consistent with this line of thinking, deviant behavior results when social controls are weakened to the point that individuals are no longer motivated to conform to established rules.

One example of a social control theory is *Containment Theory*. Proponents assert that individuals resist societal pressures encouraging a propensity toward criminality because social control, primarily fear of punishment, stressed positive self-images and goals for the future in lieu of deviant behavior. In other words, people are afraid of social penalties and, therefore, conform. They are contained by their fears and opt for more traditionally acceptable behavior.

The *Social Bond Theory* is another example. Proponents assert that crime is the result of shattered social bonds to the point where people no longer have a personal stake in conformity. According to this theory, people are not afraid of punishment per se, but the impact of their behavior on primary groups like friends, family members, and co-workers. In other words, citizens are controlled in society by the relationships they form with others. When those relationships do not exist or no longer exist, they lose their impetus to conform and lean toward criminality.

Lesson Three: Modern Critical Theories

Critical theories in criminological thinking arose in direct conflict with the American mythology of the mid-twentieth century. Americans were becoming increasingly more skeptical of the doctrine of functionalism discussed in the last chapter, whereby societal functions are compared to human bodily functions rendering each part a sub-part of the whole healthy unit. In the United States, not all social institutions were healthy. The Vietnam War, the specter of racism, political policies akin to imperialism, gender inequality, and economic disparity were just some segments of society in great need of reform. Contrarily, the mythology of the populace tended to support functionalist belief in a governmental utilitarian approach to acting in the best interests of its citizens in the face of growing evidence the opposite was true. Within American social structure, neither determinism nor free will adequately described the actions of the masses that had submitted to government control for decades. Thus, critical theories, basically sociological in nature, sprang up to offer alternative theories for voluntary submission of people to societal institutions.

Criminologists and sociologists recognize the reality of American-type democracies – by definition there is a large minority. Nevertheless, social institutions dominate the human beings that create them. Therefore, social institutions neither determine the actions of people in society, nor become subject to the free will of its citizens. Classical and positivist theories that assume societal consensus in the formulation of a working mythology did not appear to produce resolutions to the societal needs of the 1960s. This common impression spawned the belief that social institutions actually operate in conflict with one another over the establishment of societal norms and values. In fact, to critical theorists, conflict among social institutions is the norm.

Unlike sociological theories, critical theories focus on society as the unit of analysis, not the individuals comprising society. These theories have been heavily influenced by the early economic and ecological theories. In a nutshell, to critical theorists, crime is considered a label attached to behavior of the less powerful and influential in society for the purpose of protecting the interests of the more influential and powerful in society. Not coincidentally, critical theories that gained prominence in the 1960s suggest crime is a rational response to the inequitable conditions that are a by-product of a capitalist society.

Conflict Theory

Consistent with critical criminological approaches, conflict theories do not assume consensus among societal groups. Conflict criminologists view societies as characteristic of the struggle for dominance among competing groups and institutions. White versus black, rich versus poor, male versus female, and conservative versus liberal is thought to more accurately describe the evolution of American culture than the naïve submission to government characteristic of the 1950s. Of course, domination by one group presupposes subordination by another. Following this rationale and applying it to crime, it becomes more likely that dominant groups would label some actions of subordinate groups as deviant, while simultaneously considering the actions of their own dominant groups as normal. Therefore, criminal law becomes a mechanism by which dominant members of society exert control over subordinate members of the same society.

While on the surface it might appear as though all members of American society have common interests, critical theorists assert the opposite reality. Dominant societal groups exploit subordinate groups to achieve their own goals and further their own interests. Thus, to critical theorists, social position has more to do with criminality than does deviant behavior. Those not in control are deemed criminal because their social interests conflict with those in control. Crime, therefore, is a *function* of societal status.

Labeling Theory

Labeling theories are concerned with the process known as *criminalization.* Unlike classical and positivist theories that focus upon crimes and criminals respectively, labeling theoretical approaches assume that societies designate segments of the population as deviant.

One of the earliest proponents of this approach was George Herbert Mead (1863-1931). Mead asserted that human beings react to situations based upon the meanings those situations hold for them. People, therefore, find different meanings in the same actions and react according to the meaning they assign to the action. According to this approach, societal reaction is a matter of perception. Societal perceptions arise from the social interactions among human beings. Thus, perceivers of the criminal actions interpret those actions differently.

Howard Becker (1928-   ) asserted that interpretive social groups establish the rules and definitions of deviant behavioral patterns and label societal members who break those rules accordingly. Criminals are deemed outsiders and become stigmatized by the labels they are assigned. This self-fulfilling prophecy creates the impression among the labeled deviants that they are what society believes they are and therefore, act accordingly. While the theory might exaggerate the significance of labeling, there is little doubt that American society's treatment of stereotypical criminals differs greatly from the same treatment afforded to the conforming majority.

Radical Criminological Theory

Like the early economic theories previously discussed in this text, modern radical criminological theories are based largely on the anti-capitalistic views of Karl Marx. In a nutshell, radical criminologists suggest capitalism as the root cause of criminal behavior in society. Marxist theory assumes conflict among social classes, established by the individual's relationship to the mode of production of material goods. Societal members are seen as wealthy ruling classes owning the means of production in conflict with the working classes producing material goods, but receiving less than their proportionate share of the resulting wealth. Capitalist ruling classes are believed to manipulate social institutions to further their own ends, which invariably includes a greater share of societal wealth. The *haves* in capitalist economic structures are believed by radical theorists to take advantage of the *have-nots.* The resulting economic disparity, they assert, forces the lower economic classes into criminal activity to attain parity.

Radical theorists believe individual competition for economic gain encourages crime. In a sense, they assert a deterministic philosophy compelling lower economic social classes to resort to violent struggles to acquire basic human rights. Marxists believe reductions in class struggles diminish criminal activity. To accomplish this end, radical criminologists suggest new definitions of crime, all of which indicate that crime should be defined in terms of basic human rights like food, shelter, and clothing. To Marxists, capitalism fits the definition of crime since it promotes competition for wealth and power, which deprives human segments of society of their basic needs. Thus, radical theorists target capitalism as an exploitation of the working classes by the rich and powerful.

While the United States today widely rejects Marxism, it is important to understand the relationship of radical theories to socialism. Marxism is a socialist philosophy that directly attacks capitalist thinking. Socialism, however, blends sufficiently well with capitalism so as to co-exist in the same society where proponents of each can work toward common goals. American welfare, farm subsidies, Social Security, and Medicare are examples of socialist programs aimed at improving the U.S capitalist society. Like Marxism, socialism distributes wealth without economic competition. Unlike Marxism, socialism synthesizes into capitalist societies without the need to destroy them. Nevertheless, socialism forms one of the building blocks of Marxism that radical criminologists argue is the answer to the crime problem caused by capitalist economic policies.

Unfortunately, in 2019, Marxist thinking is establishing a foothold in the greatest world economy of capitalist United States of America, which might be drastically altered in the future, if the radical ideas of Karl Marx continue to infiltrate American thinking. History disputes the application of radical criminological theories as a benefit to free societies.

Conclusion: A Synthesis

The real difficulty in assessing crime causation in the twenty-first century lies neither in the abundance of criminological theories advanced, nor in the failure of criminologists to identify the singular cause of deviant behavior. The problem lies in philosophical perception – the mythology of the American people.

Philosophically speaking, large segments of American society hold diametrically opposite views from which to examine criminal activity. Consider, for example, the question of morality. When philosophers refer to this concept, they mean ethics, or the study of morality. The manner in which people should treat one another and expect to be treated by each other has been debated since ancient Greece. Morality is always the subject of controversy because it means different things to different people since the foundations of ethical beliefs differ.

Consequentialists measure human ethical actions by the consequences they produce. Non-consequentialists look to rules such as laws or religious doctrines to determine the morality of human behavior. Similarly, free will advocates assume criminal actors have control over the decisions they make so they seek to hold them accountable accordingly. Determinists, on the other hand, believe outside factors control criminal behavior and should be considered in the accountability process. Absolutists believe there is one right action for all members of society, whereas relativists claim morality depends on the time, place, and actor.

It is quite evident that societal vantage point has much to do with crime. Should a person adhere to the social problems perspective, he or she would tend to promote social programs to cure societal ills. Should a person adhere to the social responsibility perspective, he or she would tend to promote stiffer sentencing and more prisons to punish the individual offender. Thus, the mythology of the American people determines what is to be considered deviant behavior in the United States. While we might agree on a variety of acceptable social norms, we will never find unanimity of perspective. This helps to explain why the determination of crime causation is constantly in flux.

For centuries, criminologists sought singular answers to crime causation and singular solutions to crime problems in America. As we proceed through the twenty-first century, the shift in approach is overwhelmingly in favor of the multidisciplinary nature of crime theories. Nevertheless, we are still left with incompatible philosophical beliefs as tools with which to tackle the crime problem. Knowledge of the multifaceted approach is helpful in understanding the perspective of the theorist, the theoretical concept advanced, and the usefulness of the proposed theory.

In an attempt to highlight the broad philosophical parameters presented in this mini course, a summary of the major philosophical approached is in order, with the clear admonition that modern theorists combine those theories that remain compatible so as to form interdisciplinary conclusions as to crime causation and prevention.

The classical school was among the first of the early dominant theories to affect American society. The classical approach was a welcomed change from those systems based on the concept of criminal laws with supernatural origins. During the eighteenth century Age of Enlightenment, Cesare Beccaria focused on the inconsistent and brutal nature of crime punishment, advocating the concept of free will. He suggested a reasonable relationship between punishment and crime as a method of controlling criminal activity. Jeremy Bentham promoted utilitarianism in classical school fashion, suggesting that acts be judged by the greatest amount of good they provide to the greatest number of people, not by inflexible absolutist theories. Neoclassicists proved even more flexible, allowing for mitigating circumstances to be considered before imposition of punishment for crime.

The positivist school rejected the notion of free will in favor of determinism. Positivists reacted to the harsh inflexibility of the classical school, preferring a more scientific approach to crime control. They believed punishment should fit the criminal, not the crime, since they rejected the free will of the criminal actor. Cesare Lombroso, applying positivist theory, concluded that criminals differ biologically from non-criminals based on a variety of factors, including heredity, mental defects, and physical deformities. Concepts like indeterminate sentencing and judicial discretion in punishment application stem from positivism. Sigmund Freud and others suggested psychological approaches to crime causation. Supporters of this school of thought reject environmental factors, but accept mental and emotional disorders as predictors of crime.

Sociological theories emanate from Emil Durkheim. Like the positivists, he rejected the free will concept, but adopted the anomie or normlessness concept to explain deviant behavior. Robert K. Merton's strain theories, Edwin Sutherland's social process theories such as differential association, social control theories like containment and social bond concepts, and Cloward and Ohlin's differential opportunity theory all evolve from the sociological perspective on crime.

Finally, critical theories such as labeling theory advanced by Howard Becker, conflict theories, and radical criminological approaches based largely on Marxist economic principles have all been advocated as viable vantage points from which to view crime causation and solutions.

While the incompatibility of some of the above approaches is obvious, the compatibility of some other approaches is equally obvious. It is upon this principle that twenty-first century criminologists are building the new vision for future generations in hopes of nurturing a better society. By synthesizing the compatible theories to form new ones, the science of criminology is perpetuated for posterity. Experimentation with novel approaches is of paramount importance to the maintenance of a peaceful American community in the next century. Yet, we know there is no singular solution. The answer lies in acceptance of the best ideologies to flow from the process. In the long run, America's best hope for a crime-free existence lies in the adherence to a dominant mythology toward crime that considers many angles from the most collectively intelligent perspectives available. Balancing societal needs with individual rights has always been an American challenge. Merging the best researched methodologies into a unified mythology might preserve the democratic principles of our republic for centuries to come.

About the Author

JJ Botta is a freelance writer and college professor. His resume contains numerous magazine and online publications on a variety of topics. He is the author of eighteen books in the fields of Writing and the Humanities. He resides with his wife in Palm Coast, Florida.

Other Works by This Author Include:

Better Writing, Better Job: A Simple Guide to Rapid Improvement of Written Communication Skills

Perspectives of an Ordinary Man: Snapshots of Life

Are Your Beliefs Logical? THINK for a Better Life

A Hemingway Legacy: The Creative Nonfiction Memoir

Surviving the Journey: A Universal Approach for the Student Critic

Ernest Hemingway's A Moveable Feast: A Study in the Genre of Memoir

Roots of Buddhism in Pre-Communist China

7 Writing Tricks for the Clueless! Magical Improvement of Writing Skills

Criminological Theories & Theorists: An American
       Social Perspective on Crime
Murder on My Mind: Short Story Homicides
Theft: Progressive Ravaging of the American Dream
High School Lesson Plans Teachers Can Actually Use!
       Language Arts
Basic Lesson Plans for the High School Substitute
       Teacher: Language Arts
To Hug an Angel: A Foreign Adoption Nightmare
You Know What's in the Book, So Find It:
       An Easy Way to Read Literature

Online Publications Include:

"Philosophy and Contemporary Issues"

"Free Speech and Pornography"

"The Responsibility of Criminals"

"Rationalism v. Empiricism"

Further Reading

Bernard, Thomas J., et al. *Vold's Theoretical Criminology.*
New York: Oxford University Press, 2015.

Hall, Steve and Simon Winlow, eds. *New Directions in
Criminological Theory.* London and New York:
Routledge, 2012.

Higgins, George E. and Catherine D. Marcum.
Criminological Theory. New York: Wolters Kluwer,
2016.

Jung, C. G. *The Archetypes and the Collective
Unconscious.* 2nd ed. Princeton, NJ: Princeton
University Press, 1968.

McLaughlin, Eugene and Tim Newburn, eds.
Criminological Theory. London: Sage, 2010.

Tibbetts, Stephen G. and Craig Hemmens. *Criminological
Theory.* Los Angeles: Sage, 2010.